3rd Grade

TE
READING
TEST
PREP

for

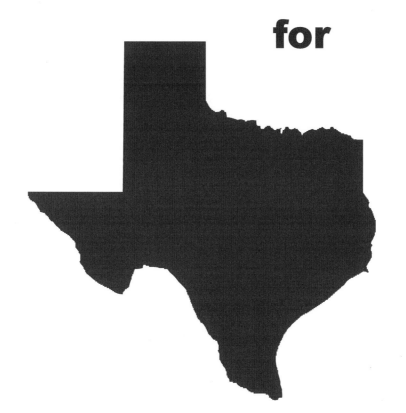

STAAR

INTRODUCTION

This resource is not intended to be another worksheet to be given to students as a STAAR review. It is the intent of the authors that the questions be used to assess and manage students' understanding of the concepts assessed on the STAAR test.

There are at least 3 questions for each TEKS. We recommend that you create a page made up of questions from three different STAAR reporting categories. The answers can serve as a diagnostic tool to determine WHY the student had an incorrect answer. The answer to the student's misunderstanding is NOT another worksheet, but a re-teaching of the skill, using different instructional strategies.

The reason for incorrect answers is often the result of the student using an incorrect procedure. Most of the errors we see as teachers are the same each year. Students apply a rule in an inappropriate way. Many times they will even say to us, "That's what you said to do." They see logic in the way they have applied the rule even though it is incorrect. Therefore, it is imperative to determine WHY a student chose an incorrect answer to a question. The best way to determine this is to ask the student to explain their solution to you.

All questions in this product are aligned to the current STAAR reporting categories and the Texas Essential Knowledge and Skills, and reflect test items from 2012-2013 STAAR tests.

3rd Grade Reading

FOR

STAAR

Table of Contents

GRADE 3 READING
Eligible TEKS for Assessment for *STAAR*

Reporting Category 1:
Understanding Across Genres

The student will demonstrate an ability to understand a variety of written texts across reading genres.

(4) Reading/Vocabulary Development. **Students understand new vocabulary and use it when reading and writing. Students are expected to**

(A) **identify the meaning of common prefixes (e.g., *in-*, *dis-*) and suffixes (e.g., *-full*, *-less*), and know how they change the meaning of roots;** *Readiness Standard*

(B) **use context to determine the relevant meaning of unfamiliar words or distinguish among multiple meaning words and homographs;** *Readiness Standard*

(C) **identify and use antonyms, synonyms, homographs, and homophones.**
Supporting Standard

Reporting Category 2:
Understanding and Analysis of Literary Texts

The student will demonstrate an ability to understand and analyze literary texts.

(2) Reading/Beginning Reading/Strategies. **Students comprehend a variety of texts drawing on useful strategies as needed. Students are expected to**

(B) **ask relevant questions, seek clarification, and locate facts and details about stories and other texts and support answers with evidence from text.** *Supporting Standard*

(5) Reading/Comprehension of Literary Text/Theme and Genre. **Students analyze, make inferences and draw conclusions about theme and genre in different cultural, historical, and contemporary contexts and provide evidence from the text to support their understanding. Students are expected to**

(A) **paraphrase the themes and supporting details of fables, legends, myths, or stories.** *Supporting Standard*

(6) Reading/Comprehension of Literary Text/Poetry. **Students understand,**

i

make inferences and draw conclusions about the structure and elements of poetry and provide evidence from text to support their understanding. Students are expected to

(A) describe the characteristics of various forms of poetry and how they create imagery (e.g., narrative poetry, lyrical poetry, humorous poetry, free verse). *Supporting Standard*

(8) Reading/Comprehension of Literary Text/Fiction. **Students understand, make inferences and draw conclusions about the structure and elements of fiction and provide evidence from text to support their understanding. Students are expected to**

(A) sequence and summarize the plot's main events and explain their influence on future events; *Readiness Standard*

(B) describe the interaction of characters including their relationships and the changes they undergo. *Readiness Standard*

(9) Reading/Comprehension of Literary Text/Literary Nonfiction. **Students understand, make inferences and draw conclusions about the varied structural patterns and features of literary nonfiction and respond by** providing evidence from text to support their understanding. *Supporting Standard*

(10) Reading/Comprehension of Literary Text/Sensory Language. **Students understand, make inferences and draw conclusions about how an author's sensory language creates imagery in literary text and provide evidence from text to support their understanding. Students are expected to**

   (A) **identify language that creates a graphic visual experience and appeals to the senses.** *Supporting Standard*

(16) Reading/Media Literacy. **Students use comprehension skills to analyze how words, images, graphics, and sounds work together in various forms to impact meaning. Students will continue to apply earlier standards with greater depth in increasingly more complex texts.** *Supporting Standard*

(Figure 19) Reading/Comprehension Skills. **Students use a flexible range of metacognitive reading skills in both assigned and independent reading to understand an author's message. Students will continue to apply earlier standards with greater depth in increasingly more complex texts as they become self-directed, critical readers. The student is expected to**

   (D) **make inferences about text and use textual evidence to support understanding;** *Readiness Standard* **(Fiction) /** *Supporting Standard* **(Literary Nonfiction, Poetry)**

   (E) **summarize information in text, maintaining meaning and logical order.** *Readiness Standard* **(Fiction) /** *Supporting Standard* **(Literary Nonfiction, Poetry)**

Reporting Category 3:
Understanding and Analysis of Informational Texts

The student will demonstrate an ability to understand and analyze informational texts.

(12) Reading/Comprehension of Informational Text/Culture and History. **Students analyze, make inferences and draw conclusions about the author's purpose in cultural, historical, and contemporary contexts and provide evidence from the text to support their understanding.**

The student expectation for 12(A) is ineligible for assessment. Therefore, when Culture and History (12) is assessed, it will be linked to Figure 19(D): *make inferences about text and use textual evidence to support understanding.* This student expectation will be attached only to expository texts, since persuasive reading is ineligible at grade 3. For this reason, Culture and History (12) will always represent a Readiness standard.

(13) Reading/Comprehension of Informational Text/Expository Text. **Students analyze, make inferences and draw conclusions about expository text and provide evidence from text to support their understanding. Students are expected to**

(A) identify the details or facts that support the main idea;
Readiness Standard

(B) draw conclusions from the facts presented in text and support those assertions with textual evidence; *Readiness Standard*

(C) identify explicit cause and effect relationships among ideas in texts;
Readiness Standard

(D) use text features (e.g., bold print, captions, key words, italics) to locate information and make and verify predictions about contents of text. *Readiness Standard*

(15) Reading/Comprehension of Informational Text/Procedural Texts. **Students understand how to glean and use information in procedural texts and documents. Students are expected to**

(B) locate and use specific information in graphic features of text.
Supporting Standard

(16) Reading/Media Literacy. **Students use comprehension skills to analyze how words, images, graphics, and sounds work together in various forms to impact meaning. Students will continue to apply earlier standards with greater depth in increasingly more complex texts.**
Supporting Standard

iv

(Figure 19) Reading/Comprehension Skills. **Students use a flexible range of metacognitive reading skills in both assigned and independent reading to understand an author's message. Students will continue to apply earlier standards with greater depth in increasingly more complex texts as they become self-directed, critical readers. The student is expected to**

(D) make inferences about text and use textual evidence to support understanding; *Readiness Standard*

(E) summarize information in text, maintaining meaning and logical order.
Readiness Standard

16. Which of the following is the BEST summary of paragraphs 8 through 10?

A   Animals use their teeth to eat other animals they have killed. They eat insects, plants, and other animals. Their teeth can grow very long during their lifetime.

B   Beavers use their teeth to build dams. Tigers use their teeth to kill. Dogs and cats use their teeth to fight. Horses, cows, and deer use their teeth to eat plants.

C   Animals have only one set of teeth. They can grow to be very long if the animals do not wear them down. Most animals use their teeth to fight and eat. Animal teeth are not like human teeth.

D   Animals use their teeth to do many jobs. The teeth may be used to kill, build homes, fight, and eat. Their teeth continue to grow all during their lives, but they do not become too long because the animals wear them down.

17. Which BEST tells the theme of paragraph 6?

A   Human teeth are important.

B   Humans have a set of temporary teeth that are replaced by permanent teeth.

C   Baby teeth last six years.

D   Humans get their first set of teeth at about six or seven months of age and   retain those teeth for about six years.

18. What is the main idea of this article?

    A   All humans, animals, and reptiles have teeth.

    B   Human and animal teeth are alike.

    C   Teeth cause many problems.

    D   Teeth are very important to humans, animals, and reptiles.

19. After humans get their first set of teeth, they

    A   get "baby teeth"

    B   get a set of permanent teeth

    C   get teeth grown in a laboratory

    D   get false teeth

20. What is the main idea of paragraph 5?

    A   Human teeth are different sizes and shapes.

    B   Humans have permanent teeth because they eat raw meat.

    C   Wisdom teeth are needed when humans eat meat.

    D   Human teeth are sharp and pointed.

Reporting Category - 3.2.B, Fig 19D
21. How do snakes USE the venom in their fangs?

A   To help them swim

B   To help the young snakes come out of the eggs

C   To make people afraid of them

D   To kill or cripple their victim

Reporting Category - 3.2.B, Fig 19D
22. A person might have his teeth pulled because

A   his teeth are too sharp

B   his teeth are causing problems

C   dental implants are better

D   scientists are growing new teeth

Reporting Category - 3.2.B, Fig 19D
23. From what the reader learns about teeth, which statement could be REASONABLE?

A   If humans take care of their teeth, they will last many years.

B   Scientists will soon give up trying to grow teeth.

C   Animal teeth are becoming stronger than human teeth.

D   More reptiles are growing a second set of teeth each year.

Reporting Category - 3.12

24. What is the author's purpose in "Teeth—what do they really do?"?

A   To entertain the reader

B   To make the reader afraid

C   To explain facts to the reader

D   To convince the reader that teeth are dangerous

Reporting Category - 3.13.D

25. Why does the author divide the article into titled sections?

A   To help the reader decide what to read

B   To organize the information in the article

C   To divide the article into equal parts

D   To make the article look interesting

Reporting Category - 3.15.B

26. Why does the author include drawings in the article?

A   To make each page nicer to look at

B   To demonstrate the purpose of teeth

C   To give the reader something to look at while reading the article

D   To illustrate facts presented in the article

27. To find this same kind of information in a library, where should you look?

A   In the card catalogue under "animal teeth"

B   In a wildlife magazine

C   In a dictionary under "teeth"

D   In an encyclopedia under "teeth"

28. Where did this article MOST LIKELY appear?

A   Atlas

B   Biography

C   Science magazine

D   Book of poetry

29. If you wanted to learn more about animal teeth, what would be the BEST thing to do?

A   Search the internet for "animal teeth"

B   Talk to a dentist

C   Write to a veterinarian

D   Look in a dictionary under "animal teeth"

30. Look at the web about human teeth. Which of these belongs in the empty circle?

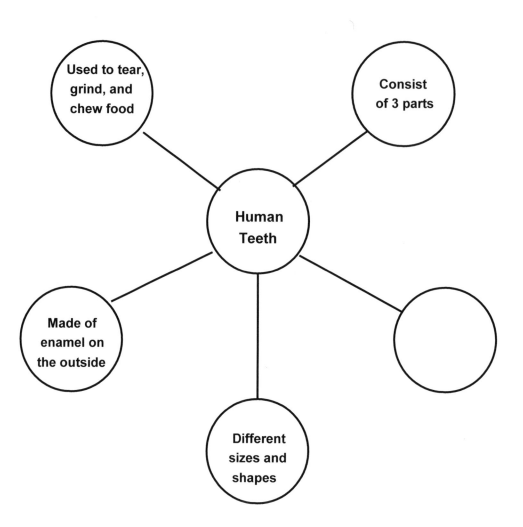

A   Same size and shape

B   Each do different jobs

C   Grown in laboratories

D   Replace false teeth

31. Look at the diagram of information from the article. Which of the following belongs in the empty box?

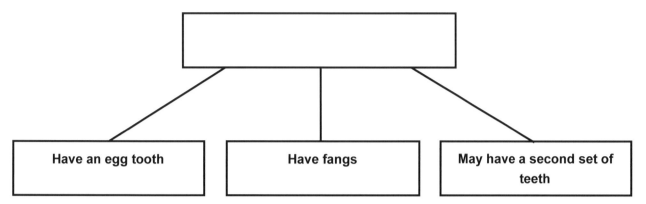

   A   Beavers

   B   Animals

   C   Humans

   D   Reptiles

Reporting Category - 3.13.A

32. Look at the diagram about human teeth and animal teeth. Which of the following goes in the blank?

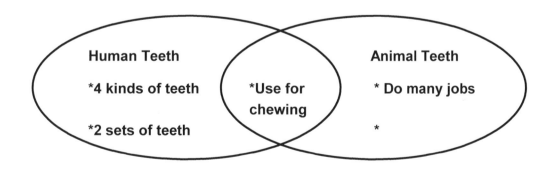

   A   Have second set   C   Keep growing

   B   32 in all   D   Have false teeth

33. Which is a FACT in this article?

    A   Today wisdom teeth are not needed, so many humans have them taken out.

    B   Humans have two sets of teeth during their lives.

    C   Dental implants could replace false teeth in the future.

    D   They have been successful in growing mice teeth.

34. Which is an OPINION in this article?

    A   Scientists are trying to grow human teeth in their laboratories.

    B   Adult humans have 32 teeth.

    C   Humans have four kinds of teeth.

    D   Wisdom teeth are no longer needed.

35. Which of these is an OPINION in this article?

    A   Scientists have been successful in growing mice teeth.

    B   Teeth are made of enamel on the outside and dentine on the inside.

    C   The teeth on the right side of the jaw are identical to the teeth on the left side.

    D   Each tooth consists of three parts.

Reporting Category - 3.4.B, Fig 19D
19. Which sentence BEST tells what the story is about?

    A   A sister discovers her brother wants a puppy.

    B   A boy and his sister share a new puppy.

    C   A boy wants a new puppy to play with during the summer.

    D   A boy's sister sees a sign about free puppies.

Reporting Category - 3.16
20. Based on information on the sign, how many puppies had been given away BEFORE Matthew called the lady?

    A   2

    B   4

    C   6

    D   3

Reporting Category - 3.2.B
21. The author MOST LIKELY mentions Matthew's dog that died to show

    A   Matthew likes male dogs

    B   Matthew likes to play with dogs

    C   Matthew knows how to care for a dog

    D   Matthew will share his new puppy with his sister

Reporting Category - 3.4.B, Fig 19D

22. Why was Matthew's father MOST LIKELY concerned the puppies might have all been given away?

    A   There were only 6 puppies, and they were a mixed breed.

    B   The puppies were free and black and white.

    C   The puppies would only be given to good homes.

    D   There were only 6 puppies, and they were free.

Reporting Category - 3.4.B, Fig 19D

23 Why did Amanda show the sign to Matthew?

    A   Matthew's father had promised him he could have a new puppy.

    B   Matthew's dog had died during the winter.

    C   The puppies were free.

    D   She wanted to play a joke on Matthew.

Reporting Category - 3.2.B

23. How is the puppy Matthew chose DIFFERENT from the other puppies?

    A   He is white.

    B   He has big brown eyes.

    C   He has a black tipped tail.

    D   He likes to play

24. The mother dog probably licked Matthew's hand because

A   he liked her puppy

B   she liked him

C   she was hungry

D   she could understand human words

25. What happened BEFORE Matthew played with the two puppies?

A   He became sad.

B   He chose the white puppy with one black spot.

C   His father told him the white puppy with one black spot was a male.

D   He woke up the sleeping puppies.

26. Matthew grew sad for the mother dog because

A   his mother had left him

B   she was upset

C   he thought animals might have human feelings

D   his dog had died

Reporting Category - 3.2.B
27. How long will Matthew have to attend school BEFORE summer vacation?

   A   3 weeks

   B   3 days

   C   2 weeks

   D   4 weeks

Reporting Category - 3.5.A
28. What was the MOST important lesson Matthew learned from his father in the story?

   A   You should never take home the first puppy you see.

   B   If you make a promise to someone, you should keep it.

   C   You should always share your pets with your sister.

   D   You should call before you go to see free puppies.

Reporting Category - 3.10.A
29. Which word describes BOTH Matthew and Amanda?

   A   Forgiving

   B   Envious

   C   Caring

   D   Selfish

Reporting Category - 3.2.B
30. Which sentence from the story shows the reader Amanda was also excited about the possibility of getting a new puppy?

    A   *Their father could not open his car door because Matthew and Amanda were leaning in the window and both talking at once.*

    B   *He heard his sister, Amanda, calling his name and he turned around.*

    C   *Without delay, Matthew, Amanda, and their father drove to the lady's house.*

    D   *Matthew picked up the little puppy he had chosen and handed him to Amanda.*

Reporting Category - 3.8.B
31. How did Matthew change AFTER he wrote down the number to call for the free puppies?

    A   *He wanted a puppy, but he decided a puppy was too much responsibility.*

    B   *He wanted a puppy for himself, but he decided to give the puppy to Amanda.*

    C   *He was excited about the free puppies, but became worried.*

    D   *He felt sad thinking about Hercules and became angry with his father.*

Reporting Category - 3.8.B
32. Information in the story suggests Matthew

    A   is older than Amanda

    B   will share the responsibilities of a new puppy with Amanda

    C   will choose a name for the new puppy

    D   wanted more than one puppy

33. What is the MAIN reason the author includes a copy of the sign in the story?

    A   To explain why Amanda and Matthew were happy after reading the sign

    B   To convince the reader to get a puppy

    C   To tell about the new puppies and their mother

    D   To describe the puppies

34. What does the author do to make sure this story entertains?

    A   Uses pictures

    B   Tells about a real boy and his sister

    C   Tells about a boy, his sister, and a new puppy

    D   Has a sad story with a happy ending

35. The author makes this story interesting to read by doing all of the following EXCEPT which one?

    A   Includes pictures of the characters

    B   Includes pictures of all of the puppies

    C   Tells a story that could be true

    D   Tells a story about puppies

Reporting Category - 3.6

36. The story about Matthew and Amanda is

A   nonfiction

B   a biography

C   an autobiography

D   fiction

Reporting Category - 3.6.A

37. How do you know "The Puppy Who Chose Matthew" is not a poem?

A   It is not written in verses.

B   It is about fictional characters.

C   It has pictures.

D   It is about animals.

Reporting Category - 3.5.A

38. Which experience would BEST help a reader to understand the theme of this story?

A   Playing with a puppy

B   The death of a pet

C   Raising a puppy

D   Having a sister

Reporting Category - 3.8.A
39. Read the chart below. It shows the order in which some events happened in the story. Which of these belongs in the empty box?

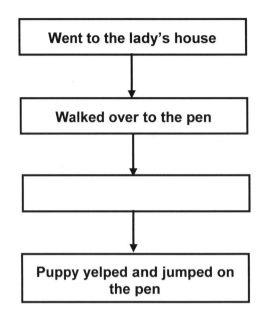

A   Greeted by a puppy   C   Played with other puppies

B   Chose Matthew   D   Chose a puppy

Reporting Category - 3.2.B
40. Look at the diagram of information from the article. Which information belongs in the blank?

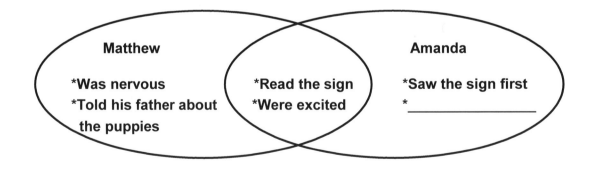

A   Chose a puppy   C   Told her father about the puppies

B   Woke up the sleeping puppies   D   Called about the free puppies

41. Which is an OPINION in this selection?

A   One day Matthew and his sister were walking home from school.

B   There were only three weeks of school left before summer vacation.

C   Today the weather was warm with a gentle breeze blowing through the tall trees.

D   Matthew opened the gate to the pen and walked over to where the other two little puppies were sleeping.

42. Which is a FACT in this selection?

A   The puppy was white with one black circle on its back, and the tip of its tail was also black.

B   They were also white, but their backs were covered with black spots.

C   You're the best brother ever.

D   But now the real work begins.

43. Which is a FACT in this selection?

A   The mother dog was not very large, had big, soft brown eyes, floppy ears, and a curly tail.

B   His best friend, a collie dog named "Hercules", had died during the winter.

C   He squatted down and put his hand on the mother dog's head.

D   Matthew and Amanda ran home as fast as they could.

44. How is Matthew's puppy DIFFERENT from the other two puppies?

A   Matthew's puppy is white.

B   Matthew's puppy is a male.

C   Matthew's puppy has lots of energy.

D   Matthew's puppy lives in a pen.

45. How are Matthew and Amanda ALIKE?

A   They go to the same school.

B   They are looking forward to summer vacation.

C   They had a dog who died.

D   They can read.

Which of the following is TRUE of Matthew's father?

A   He works in a city.

B   He liked the female puppies better than the male puppy.

C   He wants Matthew to get a puppy.

D   He was afraid Matthew would not choose a good puppy.

Dear Diary

1   Jason has kept a diary of his experiences since he was in the second grade. He enjoys going back and reading the daily <u>entries</u>. Sometimes he is reminded of events that he has forgotten about. Many times he starts to laugh or smile when he reads about the many different <u>incidents</u> that have happened to him. Some days are more exciting to read about than others. Two of his favorite entries are March 10 and July 4.

March 10

Dear Diary,

2   I had a very exciting day today. This morning my mother asked me to go with her to the mall. When we got there, I remembered that my favorite football player, Tony Romo, would be signing autographs today at a sporting goods store. I wanted to get his autograph, but we had to do our errands first.

3   First, we went to the drugstore to pick up some medicine for my grandmother. Our next stop was the greeting card shop. My father has a birthday next week, and my mother wanted to buy him a special card. We searched for just the right card, and finally found a card with a man hitting a golf ball on the front. My dad likes to play golf with his friends from work, so we thought he would really like it.

4   We were hungry so we decided to eat lunch in the food <u>court</u>. We looked at the different choices of food. Both of us thought the pizza looked and smelled good. I ate two pieces of cheese pizza, and my mom ate one piece of pepperoni pizza.

5   We then went to the sporting goods store to find Tony Romo, but when we got there I saw a sign that said, "Gone to lunch. Be back in one hour." I was devastated because I knew my mother did not have time to wait an hour. She said, "I am so sorry we missed your hero. Maybe he will come again, and we will come to see him then." I was so disappointed that I just hung my head and followed her out of the store.

6   As we were walking to our car, a sport utility vehicle pulled up to the curb and a man got out. He was very large and was carrying a large bag. I looked at him, and he looked at me. I was shocked when I realized I was looking at Tony Romo. I said, "Hello, Mr. Romo." He said, "Hi, pal. Did you come for an autograph?" My mom heard our <u>conversation</u> and stopped walking to our car. She came back to where I was standing. I was so excited I could not answer him. My mom came to my <u>rescue</u> and said, "Yes, we did!"

7   Well, as you might guess, I got my autograph. But even better than that, I got to talk to Tony Romo. Now I know why he is my favorite football player. Not only is he a great football player, but he is a very nice man.

Jason B.

July 4

Dear Diary,

8   Today was a very special day! This is a day when Americans celebrate their <u>freedom</u> and independence from England. Most people spend the day with their families and friends.   Many celebrate with barbecues, picnics, and best of all, fireworks.

9   My family spent the day with my grandparents who live on a lake. My dad fished all day, and my brother and sister swam and rode in the boat. My mom sat under a tree and visited with her relatives. I did everything! Sometimes I fished, and then I swam or rode in the boat. When we go to the lake, I never get bored or ever get to do everything I want to do. The time always passes too fast!

10   I ate so much my stomach hurt. The food was delicious. My aunts, uncles, and cousins brought sandwiches, fried chicken, potato salad, cakes, pies, cookies, and much more. I tried to eat some of everything, and the way my stomach felt, I think I did. My mom fussed at me because I always had something to eat in my hands. I could not help it. I was hungry!

11   My dad and I caught lots of fish. Well, not really lots, but some. I caught three <u>perch</u> and one catfish. My grandpa cleaned the fish and put them in the freezer. He said the next time I came for a visit, he would cook them for me. I can't wait to eat the fish I caught!

12   When it got dark, the fireworks started. A group of people who live on the lake buy fireworks every year and have a big fireworks <u>display</u>. My grandpa had bought <u>sparklers</u> for the grandkids. We had fun making designs in the air with them. The fireworks were really pretty. My favorite was red, white, and blue stars that burst all over the sky.

13   Next year I want to spend more time fishing. I think with practice I can become a really good fisherman.

Jason B.

Reporting Category - 3.4.E
1. In paragraph 8, the word <u>freedom</u> means   _____

    A   not obeying rules

    B   being able to move and act freely

    C   to depend on someone

    D   not eager

Reporting Category - 3.4.B
2. In paragraph 12, the word <u>display</u> means   _____

    A   roles in a performance

    B   explosion

    C   noise

    D   show

Reporting Category - 3.4.B
3. In paragraph 12, the word <u>sparklers</u> means   _____

    A   a firework that gives off very bright sparks as it burns

    B   flashes of light

    C   setting off

    D   games

4. In paragraph 1, which words help the reader know what <u>incidents</u> means?

    A   *a diary*

    B   *more exciting*

    C   *many different*

    D   *experiences*

5. In paragraph 6, the word <u>conversation</u> means _____

    A   laughter

    B   talking

    C   meeting

    D   whispering

6. In paragraph 6, the word <u>rescue</u> means _____

    A   side

    B   car

    C   aid

    D   friend

Reporting Category - 3.4.B

7. Read the meanings below for the word <u>court</u>.

Which meaning best fits the way <u>court</u> is used in paragraph 4?

A   Meaning 3

B   Meaning 2

C   Meaning 1

D   Meaning 4

court ('kōrt) *noun*
1. The home of a ruler.   2. A space for playing a game.   3. An open space.
4. An official meeting led by a judge.

Reporting Category - 3.4.B

8. Read the meanings below for the word <u>perch</u>.

Which meaning best fits the way <u>perch</u> is used in paragraph 11?

A   Meaning 4

B   Meaning 3

C   Meaning 2

D   Meaning 1

perch ('perch) *noun*
1. The place where birds roost.
2. A fresh water food fish.   3. A raised seat.
verb
4. To sit or rest on.

Reporting Category - 3.4.B

9. Read the meanings below for the word <u>entry</u>.

Which meaning best fits the way <u>entries</u> is used in paragraph 1?

A   Meaning 3

B   Meaning 4

C   Meaning 2

D   Meaning 1

entry ('en-trē) *noun*
1. An entrance, as a door.   2. A person or thing entered in a contest.   3. The act of going in.   4. A written record of something.

10. Paragraph 1 is mostly about _____

    A   funny experiences Jason has had

    B   Jason's favorite entries

    C   Jason's diary

    D   exciting entries

11. What is the diary entry of July 4th mostly about?

    A   Jason and his father catch fish and ride in a boat.

    B   Jason spends a day fishing, swimming, and boating with his family.

    C   Americans spend the day celebrating with barbecues, picnic, and fireworks.

    D   Jason and his family go to his grandparent's house to spend a holiday with his relatives.

12. What is the diary entry of March 10th mostly about?

    A   A boy and his mom spend the day at a mall running errands.

    B   A boy and his mom go to a mall to run errands, and while they are there they meet a famous football player.

    C   A boy and his mother go to a sports store to get an autograph.

    D   A boy and his mother buy a birthday card at a card shop and a box of golf balls at a sporting goods store.

13. Which of the following is the best summary of the March 10th diary entry?

    A   Jason and his mom go to a mall. They buy gifts and eat pizza. Jason sees his favorite football player.

    B   Tony Romo is at a sporting goods store signing autographs in the mall. Jason and his mom search for Mr. Romo, but learn that he has gone to lunch. Jason was disappointed because he would not be able to see his favorite football player at the mall.

    C   Jason and his mom go to a mall to run errands. While they are at the mall, he remembers Tony Romo is signing autographs at a sporting goods store. Jason thinks he has missed seeing his favorite football player, but spots him as they are leaving and gets his autograph.

    D   When Jason and his mom are at the mall, they go to a drugstore and eat pizza at the food court. Jason sees a football player and gets his autograph.

14. How did Jason feel when he left the mall?

    A   Concerned

    B   Discouraged

    C   Thrilled

    D   Angry

15. Which words in paragraph 1 help the reader to know how Jason feels when he reads his diary?

    A   *Kept a diary*

    B   *Sometimes he is reminded*

    C   *Favorite entries*

    D   *Laugh or smile*

16. Information in the article suggests that on July 4th, most Americans feel _____

    A   hungry

    B   proud

    C   talkative

    D   tired

17. Where did Jason spend July 4th?

    A   At a barbecue

    B   In a boat

    C   At his house

    D   At his grandparent's house

18. Where was Jason when he met Tony Romo?

    A   In a parking lot

    B   In a mall

    C   In a sports store

    D   At a football game

19. How long has Jason kept a diary?

A   Since July 4th

B   Since March 10th

C   Since the second grade

D   Two years

20. On March 10th Jason's problem was solved when he _____

A   went to the sports store

B   remembered Tony Romo would be signing autographs in the mall

C   met Tony Romo in a parking lot

D   went to the mall with his mother

21. Why did Jason's grandfather probably buy sparklers for the children?

A   They are not very expensive.

B   They are safer for children to use.

C   The children like sparklers better than fireworks.

D   They do not make a noise.

22. Jason's main problem on March 10th was that _____

    A   Tony Romo was not at the sporting goods store on the day Jason went to the mall

    B   Tony Romo refused to sign autographs during lunch

    C   Tony Romo only gives autographs to adults

    D   Tony Romo was gone when he went to get an autograph, and his mother could not wait for Mr. Romo to return

23. What happened after dark on July 4th?

    A   The children made designs with sparklers.

    B   People who live on the lake bought fireworks.

    C   Grandpa bought sparklers for the children.

    D   Jason spent the day at a lake.

24. After Jason and his mom went to the greeting card shop, they went to a _____

    A   a drugstore

    B   a pizza cafe

    C   a mall

    D   birthday party

Reporting Category - 3.2.B
25. When will Jason eat the fish he caught?

A   After it gets dark

B   On March 10th

C   Next year on July 4th

D   The next time he visits his grandparents

Reporting Category - 3.8.A
26. Read the chart below. It shows the order in which some events happened in the story.
    Which of these belongs in the empty box?

A   Was disappointed

B   Saw Tony Romo

C   Went to a drugstore

D   Ate pizza

Reporting Category - 3.2.B
27. Look at the web about July 4th. Which of these belongs in the empty circle?

A   Red, white, and blue stars

B   Celebrates freedom from England

C   Go to a mall

D   Catch fish

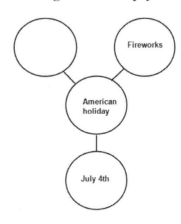

28. Look at the diagram of information from the article. Which information belongs in the blank?

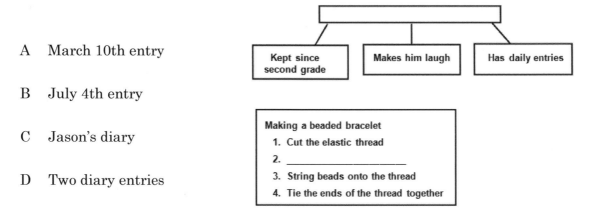

A   March 10th entry

B   July 4th entry

C   Jason's diary

D   Two diary entries

29. When Jason writes an entry in his diary, he is writing _____

A   a book

B   a story

C   a letter

D   an article

30. Why does each entry include a date?

A   It tells the reader who wrote the entry in the diary.

B   It tells the reader when the entry was written in the diary.

C   The writer must write an entry each day.

D   Each diary page has a space for the date.

Reporting Category - 3.9
31. Which paragraph is *not* part of a diary entry?

    A   Paragraph 13

    B   Paragraph 2

    C   Paragraph 8

    D   Paragraph 1

Reporting Category - 3.2.B
32. Jason's dad will probably like his birthday card because _____

    A   Jason and his mom bought it at a mall

    B   he likes to play golf

    C   it is his birthday

    D   Jason found the card

Reporting Category - 3.16.B
33. How would the ending of Jason's March 10th diary entry have changed if he had not met Tony Romo?

    A   Jason would have been tired.

    B   Jason and his mother would have returned to the mall the next day.

    C   Jason would have been very upset.

    D   Jason would no longer like Tony Romo.

Reporting Category - 3.2.B; Reporting Category – 3.16.B
34. Why was Jason probably not bored at the lake on July 4th?

    A   It was a holiday.

    B   His grandpa saved his fish.

    C   His brother and sister were with him.

    D   There are many things to do at the lake.

Reporting Category - 3.2.B
35. Which sentence from the article shows the reader that Jason likes fireworks?

    A   *When it got dark, the fireworks started.*

    B   *Many celebrate with barbecues, picnics, and best of all, fireworks.*

    C   *The fireworks were really pretty.*

    D   *My grandpa had bought sparklers for the grandkids.*

Reporting Category - 3.2.B
36. Which statement shows the reader how Jason felt when he met Tony Romo?

    A   *I said, "Hello, Mr. Romo."*

    B   *My mom heard our conversation and stopped walking to our car.*

    C   *I was so disappointed that I just hung my head and followed my mother out of the store.*

    D   *I was so excited I could not answer him.*

Erin's New Backpack

1   As Erin walked to the mailbox, she noticed dark clouds forming in the sky. The weather had been rainy all week, but the weatherman had predicted sunny skies for today. She and her mother had planned a trip to the mall if the weather cooperated. She wanted to get a new backpack before she started school.

2   Erin rushed into the house with the mail. "Mom, it looks as if a storm is brewing," Erin said to her mother. "We may have to postpone our trip to the mall."

3   When Erin handed her mother the mail, a brightly colored pamphlet fell to the floor. Erin picked it up and immediately noticed it was from a store in the mall. As she opened the pamphlet, she saw an advertisement for backpacks. She looked at all of the backpacks featured on the advertisement and felt confident she could easily find one if she went to this store.

4   Later that afternoon after the storm had passed by, Erin and her mother traveled to the shopping mall. They visited the store that had advertised the backpacks. It didn't take Erin long to find a pretty pink and green cloth backpack with large pockets on the front and back. The salesperson rang up the sale and bagged the backpack for Erin. She couldn't wait to show her friends. She just knew she had the prettiest backpack of any third grader at Crossland Elementary.

5

Erin was so proud of her backpack. It was large enough to carry all of her books, but it was still small enough not to hurt her back. Her father had told her of the danger of carrying a backpack that was too heavy. It could injure her back and cause her problems even after she became an adult.

6   Erin and her mother got home before her father arrived from work. "Erin, please come and help me carry the grocery bags into the house," her mother called from the back of the car. She and her mother had stopped at a local market and bought a few items her mother needed to prepare dinner needed to prepare dinner for the family that evening. Erin placed the bag containing the new backpack on the driveway so she could carry some bags for her mother. After all of the grocery bags were inside, Erin helped her mother put the groceries away. Erin's mother began to cook dinner while Erin watched TV.

7   Erin's family liked to discuss the day's events at their dinner table each evening. Erin couldn't wait to tell her father about her new backpack. Just as she started describing the backpack, she remembered she had left the bag with the backpack in it on the driveway. She quickly jumped up from her dining chair and exclaimed, "My backpack! I left it on the driveway. I hope nothing has happened to it."

8   Erin ran outside as fast as she could. She looked where her backpack should have been. It wasn't there! "Oh, no!" she cried. "What could have happened to my backpack?" She looked on the driveway, under the car, and in the yard. Then she put her hand over her mouth. She had a sick feeling in her stomach because she was so afraid her pretty, new backpack was gone forever.

9   Erin ran back inside sobbing and talking all at once. "My backpack is gone. I don't know what to do. I looked everywhere and it's gone," she cried.

10   "Didn't you bring it inside?" asked her mother. "I thought you went back outside to get it after we put the grocery items away," her mother said as she tried to comfort Erin. Erin thought for a moment and decided to look in the family room. Maybe she had just forgotten she had brought the backpack inside after all.

11   Erin looked on the sofa, in the chairs, on the floor near the television, and under the window, but still no backpack. She flopped down on the sofa and began to cry. Her mother came in the room and sat down beside Erin. "We'll find your backpack. If not, we'll go first thing tomorrow morning and buy another one. The store probably has another one just like the one you bought," her mother said calmly. But Erin was sure she had not seen another backpack like the one she bought. She just felt terrible!

12   Erin helped her mother clear the table and put the dishes in the dishwasher. Her brother, Paul, and her father told her they would go outside and look again. "I bet we can find it," said Paul. "I'm good at finding things. Remember when you lost your jacket, and I found it in the garage." Erin thought about what Paul said and felt a little bit better. Her brother had helped her many times when she had a problem, and this was one time when she REALLY needed his help.

13   Paul and Erin's father walked outside immediately. They looked everywhere, but the backpack was nowhere to be found.

14   All Erin could think about was her backpack. It was just the right size and her favorite colors. She began to feel sick again. If only she had not taken the backpack out of the car. She knew she should have put it in the house before she helped her mother unload their purchases. What if it was gone forever?

15   Erin thought about how long it would take for tomorrow to arrive. She was so worried about finding a backpack just like the one she had lost. As she climbed the stairs to her bedroom, she heard the doorbell ring. Her mother opened the door and began to laugh.

16   "Erin, please come here. Someone wants to see you," called her mother. As Erin walked down the stairs, she saw Mr. Mason, their neighbor, standing in the doorway holding her backpack. "Where did you find it? Is it ruined? Who had it? Was it stolen?" Erin asked excitedly. "I found it in my front yard," laughed Mr. Mason. "I guess one of the neighborhood dogs found it and carried it over to my yard. When I opened the bag, I knew it had to belong to you because pink and green are your favorite colors."

17   "Thank you, Mr. Mason," said Erin

with a big grin on her face. "I'll never leave anything lying outside again. I've learned my lesson! No matter what, I'll take better care of my things from now on."

1. What is the meaning of the word *postpone* below?

> *We may have to postpone our trip to the mall.*

A   rush

B   ride a bus

C   put off until later

D   go immediately

2. What is the meaning of the word *pamphlet* below?

> *When Erin handed her mother the mail, a brightly colored pamphlet fell to the floor.*

A   balloon

B   package

C   stamped envelope

D   printed material

3. What is the meaning of the word *confident* below?

> *She looked at all of the backpacks featured on the advertisement and felt confident she could easily find one if she went to this store.*

A   unsure

B   no doubt

C   frightened

D   delighted

4. How did Erin probably FEEL after she talked to Mr. Mason?

    A   Strange

    B   Angry

    C   Thankful

    D   Serious

5. Erin felt sick when she started looking for her new backpack because she

    A   was worried she would not find it

    B   was tired of looking everywhere

    C   thought she had left it at the mall

    D   had eaten cookies before dinner

6. What is the MOST important lesson Erin learns in the story?

    A   The mall has a large selection of backpacks.

    B   Backpacks should never be heavy.

    C   Storms don't last very long.

    D   You should always take care of your possessions.

Reporting Category - 3.2.B
7. Why did Erin BELIEVE her brother might find her backpack?

    A   His father would help him look for the backpack.

    B   He knew where to look.

    C   He had helped her at other times.

    D   He had helped her find her bike.

Reporting Category - 3.2.B
8. Why was Erin's mother NOT worried about her finding the lost backpack?

    A   She knew Paul was good at finding lost items.

    B   She had seen Erin put the backpack in the family room.

    C   She knew she could find the backpack.

    D   She believed they could buy another one.

Reporting Category - 3.2.B, Fig 19D
9. The story takes place

    A   after school had started

    B   before school began

    C   during the winter

    D   during the spring

Reporting Category - 3.2.B, Fig 19D
10. What could have been a PROBLEM for Erin?

A   The store didn't have another backpack like the one she lost.

B   The backpack was still in the car.

C   Her brother found her backpack.

D   Her mother had gone to the store to buy another backpack for Erin.

Reporting Category - 3.2.B
11. What did the author mean when he said "if the weather cooperated"?

A   If it was warm

B   If it was cold

C   If it wasn't stormy

D   If it wasn't sunny

Reporting Category - 3.2.B
12. Which of the following did Erin think might NOT have happened to the backpack?

A   It was ruined.

B   It was in her room.

C   It had been stolen.

D   Someone had it.

Reporting Category - 3.4.C
13. Which means almost the SAME as *predicted* from the sentence below?

The weather had been rainy all week, but the weatherman had predicted sunny skies for today.

A   said   C   expected

B   seen   D   commanded

Reporting Category - 3.4.C
14. When the author says the salesperson *rang up* in the sentence below, he means

The salesperson rang up the sale and bagged the backpack.

A   she wrote the amount owed on a bill

B   she called Erin on a cell phone

C   she used the cash register

D   she answered a telephone

Reporting Category - 3.4.C
15. Which pair of words from the story has almost the SAME meaning?

A   arrive, rushed

B   sobbing, cry

C   calmly, laughed

D   everywhere, outside

16. Read the meanings for the word *form*. Which meaning best fits the way *forming* is used in the sentence below?

As Erin walked to the mailbox, she noticed dark clouds forming in the sky.

A   Meaning 3

B   Meaning 2

C   Meaning 1

D   Meaning 4

> **form ('fôrm) *noun***
> **1. The shape and structure of something.   2. A printed sheet with blank spaces for information.   3. A mold in which concrete is placed to set.**
> ***verb***
> **4. To take form or come into being.**

17. Read the meanings for the word *brew*. Which meaning best fits the way *brewing* is used in the sentence below?

"Mom, it looks as if a storm is brewing," Erin said to her mother.

A   Meaning 4

B   Meaning 3

C   Meaning 2

D   Meaning 1

> **brew ('brü) *verb***
> **1. To make a beverage from water, malt, and hops.   2. To prepare by soaking in hot water.**
> **3. To plan.   4. To start to form.**

18. Read the meanings for the word *event*. Which meaning best fits the way *events* is used in the sentence below?

Erin's family liked to discuss the day's events at their dinner table each evening.

A   Meaning 3

B   Meaning 4

C   Meaning 2

D   Meaning 1

> **event (i-'vent) *noun***
> **1. Something usually of importance that happens.   2. A social occasion.**
> **3. The fact of happening.   4. A contest in a program of sports.**

19. Which sentence BEST tells what the story is about?

A   A girl is disappointed.

B   A girl is helped by her brother and father.

C   A girl likes her neighbor.

D   A girl learns a lesson.

20. What is the BEST reason Erin liked the backpack?

A   It was not expensive.

B   It was her favorite colors.

C   It had large pockets.

D   It was the prettiest backpack in Crossland Elementary.

21. Why did Erin's mother go to a market?

A   To buy Erin a backpack

B   To cook dinner

C   To buy items she needed to cook dinner

D   To visit a mall

Reporting Category - 3.8.B
22. Why was dinner a good time for Erin's family to share their experiences?

    A   They liked the same kinds of food.

    B   It was dark outside.

    C   Erin liked to tell about her new purchases.

    D   They were all present for dinner.

Reporting Category - 3.2.B
23. Why did Amanda BELIEVE she could find a backpack she liked at the store in the mall?

    A   She saw the backpack she wanted in the advertisement.

    B   The store had a large selection of backpacks.

    C   Her mother was taking her to the mall to find a backpack.

    D   She liked to shop at the mall.

Reporting Category - 3.2.B
24. Which is the BEST reason the backpack Erin chose was a good one for her?

    A   It was her favorite colors.

    B   It was at a store in the mall.

    C   It was not too large.

    D   Her mother liked the backpack.

Reporting Category - 3.2.B, Fig 19D
25. The store probably sent out a pamphlet advertising backpacks because

    A   Erin wanted a new backpack

    B   it was time for school to begin

    C   they were the only store that had backpacks for sale

    D   everyone shopped at the mall

Reporting Category - 3.8.A
26. What happened BEFORE Erin helped her mother unload the bags from the car?

    A   Erin wanted to tell her father about her new backpack.

    B   She helped her mother put the groceries away.

    C   Erin's mother began to cook dinner.

    D   Erin placed her backpack on the driveway.

Reporting Category - 3.8.B
27. Why did Erin's mother probably remain calm when Erin couldn't find her backpack?

    A   She saw Erin put the backpack inside the house.

    B   She didn't want Erin to become more upset.

    C   She didn't like the backpack.

    D   She was busy cooking dinner for her family.

Reporting Category - 3.2.B

28. WHEN will Erin go back to the mall to buy another backpack?

A   Today

B   Next week

C   Tomorrow

D   Tonight

Reporting Category - 3.2.B, Fig 19D

29. Why did Erin's mother probably laugh when she answered the doorbell?

A   Mr. Mason said something funny to her.

B   She was happy to see Erin's backpack.

C   She had found Erin's backpack.

D   She wanted Mr. Mason to look for Erin's backpack.

Reporting Category - 3.10.A

30. Which word does not describe BOTH Erin and her mother?

A   Anxious

B   Helpful

C   Happy

D   Confident

31. Which sentence from the story shows the reader Erin didn't think her backpack would be found?

    A   *Erin thought about what Paul said and felt a little better.*

    B   *Erin ran outside as fast as she could.*

    C   *She began to feel sick again.*

    D   *She looked on the driveway, under the car, and in the yard.*

32. How did Erin change AFTER Mr. Mason rang the doorbell?

    A   She was thankful.

    B   She was sad.

    C   She was afraid.

    D   She was undecided.

33. Information in the story suggests Erin

    A   is older than Paul

    B   often helps her mother

    C   is younger than Paul

    D   is irresponsible

Reporting Category - 3.16

34. What is the MAIN reason the author includes a picture of the backpack?

    A   To explain why Erin liked the backpack

    B   To show the size of the backpack

    C   To show the colors of the backpack

    D   To show more details about the backpack

Reporting Category - 3.10.A

35. What does the author do to make sure this story entertains?

    A   Uses suspense

    B   Tells about a problem

    C   Tells about a girl in the third grade

    D   Has a sad ending

Reporting Category - 3.2.B

36. The author makes this story interesting to read by doing all of the following EXCEPT which one?

    A   Includes a picture of one of the characters

    B   Shows a picture of Erin's family

    C   Tells a story that could be true

    D   Tells a story about people helping each other

Reporting Category - 3.5A
37. Which of the following is NOT a lesson the author wants the reader to learn?

A   Take care of your possessions

B   Help others

C   Shop at a mall for a backpack

D   Be appreciative when others help you

Reporting Category - 3.2.B, Fig 19D
38. The story about Erin is

A   nonfiction

B   a biography

C   an autobiography

D   fiction

Reporting Category - 3.2.B, Fig 19D
39. How do you know the story is not NONFICTION?

A   It is about a girl.

B   It is not about real people.

C   It has pictures.

D   It has paragraphs.

Reporting Category – 3.5.A
40. Which experience would BEST help a reader to understand the theme of this story?

    A   Buying a backpack

    B   Helping your mother

    C   Crying

    D   Losing something important

Reporting Category - 3.2.B
41. Look at the web about the story. Which of these belongs in the empty circle?

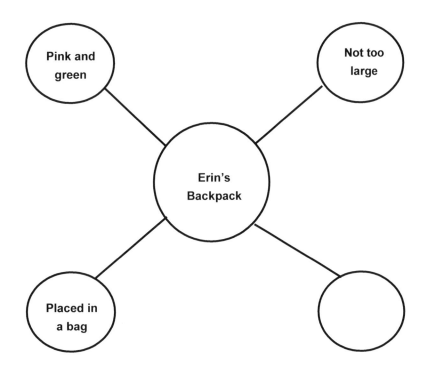

    A   Found in Erin's yard   C   Placed on the driveway

    B   Contained Erin's books   D   Was expensive

Reporting Category - 3.2.B

42. Look at the diagram of information from the article. Which information belongs in the blank?

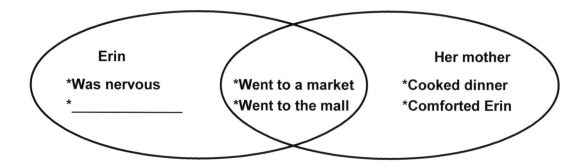

A   Sat on the sofa

C   Opened the door

B   Felt sick

D   Found Erin's jacket

Reporting Category - 3.2.B

43. Which is an OPINION in this article?

A   As she opened the pamphlet, she saw an advertisement for backpacks.

B   Erin's mother began to cook dinner while Erin watched TV.

C   Erin ran outside as fast as she could.

D   Her mother opened the door and began to laugh.

Reporting Category - 3.2.B

44. Which is a FACT in this article?

A   Erin and her mother got home before her father arrived home from work.

B   Paul and Erin's father walked outside immediately.

C   Erin rushed into the house with the mail.

D   She just knew she had the prettiest backpack of any third grader at Crossland Elementary.

45. Which of these is an OPINION in this article?

A   As she climbed the stairs to her bedroom, she heard the doorbell ring.

B   Then she put her hand over her mouth.

C   Erin looked on the sofa, in the chairs, on the floor near the television, and   under the window, but still no backpack.

D   Erin was so proud of her backpack.

ANSWER KEY

Come Ye To The Faire!

Page 5	B, C, B
Page 6	D, C, B
Page 7	A, D, A
Page 8	C, B, D
Page 9	A, C, B
Page 10	B, D, C

Sophie and the Magic Watering Can / What Happens to Christmas?

Page 14	C, B, A
Page 15	B, A, A
Page 16	D, C, A
Page 17	B, C, A
Page 18	B, C, Open
Page 19	B, D, C
Page 20	Open, C, A
Page 21	C, Open, B
Page 22	B, A, Open
Page 23	A, D, C
Page 24	Open, B, C
Page 25	Open, C, B

Teeth - What They Really Do?

Page 28	B, D, C
Page 29	C, A, D
Page 30	C, A, B
Page 31	A, C, B
Page 32	B, D, A
Page 33	D, B
Page 34	D, B, A
Page 35	D, B, A
Page 36	C, B, D
Page 37	D, C, A
Page 38	B

Page 39	D, C
Page 40	B, D, A
Page 41	C, B, A

The Puppy Who Chose Matthew

Page 45	D, B, A
Page 46	C, D, B
Page 47	B, D, C
Page 48	C, D, B
Page 49	A, D, C
Page 50	B, A, A
Page 51	B, D, C
Page 52	D, A, C
Page 53	B, D, C
Page 54	A, B, C
Page 55	A, C, B
Page 56	A, C, B
Page 57	D, A, C
Page 58	A, C
Page 59	C, A, C
Page 60	B, D, C

Dear Diary

Page 63	B, D, A
Page 64	D, B, C
Page 65	A, C, B
Page 66	C, D, B
Page 67	C, C, D
Page 68	B, D, A
Page 69	C, C, B
Page 70	D, A, B
Page 71	D, D, B
Page 72	C, C, B
Page 73	D, B, C
Page 74	D, B, D

Erin's New Backpack

Page 78	C, D, B
Page 79	C, A, D
Page 80	C, D, B
Page 81	A, C, B
Page 82	C, C, B
Page 83	D, A, A
Page 84	D, B, C
Page 85	D, B, C
Page 86	B, D, B
Page 87	C, B, A
Page 88	C, A, B
Page 89	D, A, B
Page 90	C, D, B
Page 91	D, C
Page 92	B, C, A
Page 93	D

Made in the USA
San Bernardino, CA
04 March 2015